The Constant Equilibrium

Aaron Summer Javadi

Presentation by *BookLeaf Publishing*

Web: www.bookleafpub.com

E-mail: info@bookleafpub.com

ISBN: 9789357214766

First edition 2022

ACKNOWLEDGEMENT

I'd like to thank my husband and children who have supported my efforts and work in self discovery and who have all contributed to the spiritual uplifting that has been necessary to sustain my life. I want to thank my Mother and siblings for staying beside me throughout the highs and lows met by finding the light after immense suffering in grief and loss.

I would like to thank Corinna West, who taught me how to fight for mental health advocacy and to tell my story. I would also like to thank Jessica Lowell Mason for encouraging me to embrace MAD Pride through Madwomen in the Attic and our community memoir writing projects. I would like to thank Heather Davis for her continual encouragement and guidance in spiritual matters and existential conversations through peer support.

I would like to thank Steve Nash, who assisted me with increasing informed wellness on intergenerational complex trauma therapies and awareness of child hood trauma and mental health advocacy. I would like to acknowledge Sarah Nicole Nadler for her continual efforts in sharing wisdom of writing and giving me the opportunity to gain insight into the publishing industry. I would like to thank Dr. Ann Marti Friedman for her Mentorship and wisdom in historical fiction writing and lending an ear for all my genre questions and ideas.

I am thankful for the strength that friends and family extend to me and am eternally grateful.

Gray

Have you ever stared into an ocean torrent blue
that robbed you of your peace?

Venus and her pearl has kept my lullaby, my
sleep.

Oft twilight gloom pawing,
The rest slips through
the cracks of my youth,
Each half glimpsed stair
descending down down down
into a frightened river forest round.

Cold water kissed
by the blood moon's reflection.

That's where I saw it:
Gray,
like the last ink blot left
in a puddle dot in the cup
of my bastard unwritten misfortune.

A mirror of fleeing stars
climb the winter night sky breeze,
Where vapors of breathless enchantments

scream out my Master's manhood,
From this I wished his borrowed name,
Yet he died before the freedom papers took.

I never begged for the belly of Innana.
I never asked for the red ochre of Willendorf at
my tooth.

I never screamed for the cliffs of Iona.
I never wanted for the Niles to rip tides about
my fair.

Instead of crying for my purpose.
I pitched a fit and tore my clothes off
running naked towards the unfavorable
expression of hatred for the desperate killings of
the babes left starving, some already dead in
toyland's nook.

Negroid Abolition

Inroads,
Beneath a buck moon sonnet.
Catching glimpses,
Washing away into a negroid abolition.

Hope fills the sullen vessel beside misery's
accompanied pen,
That vigorously writes a cursed release of breath
off into the sacred night,
And with it, a flittering butterfly ransom violet
blend,
An oxytocin summit lens,
Positive feedback looped liberation,
And into the nothing void I descend.

No longer concerned with the samsara noise,
selfishness has claimed me as it were,
No other entry upon my certificate at naked
birth,
I follow after the cadence,
Of a bastard's dearth,
A baby's cry, winced within,
My solemn earth.

The glow emerges,

From a destructive
Kali Emporess,
I will not render
this gollum owlet screech
a single
copper worth.

Under the Bodhi Tree

The swirl of water and bright,
Translucence of Light,
Hovering zinc green
comes down
to hug me
like a copper penny found
lost along the drain.

Fill me up
with words
And knowledge of my ancestors,
A trickling of spirits,
I catch their scent
with cotton fibered hands
strained out to repurpose.

Wrenched out to surface,
Flutter that hot air balloon
Sweep Christ through doors
Of clenched teeth
A slap to my cheek
Awakens the threat of exposure
The vodka elixir swirled bones
Cannot beat
Hard enough
against my tired

Pineal decalcified membrane.

Insane, insane, insane,
Walls, kaleidoscope figurines,
Shift between remembered scenes
Caught up in a three year old
Shift shaped little girl,
What kept her mother from pulling that trigger,
That trigger sprang loose,
Water fountain spigot games,
Fidgeting shame.
Dulce winters lost to hired hands of a Ku Klux
Klan knight,
Strangling my neck,
Bosom breast fright,
Place the brightest yellow light in my bedroom
closet filter.

Screams, screams, screams,
Through an abandoned night,
Open your eyes to see your Celtic bearded god
fall down to his knees and be shaved,
By the pink Nazi Roman flags of misfortune.
The sale block opens.

And the leaves fall
From the rain drop branches
No longer stirred by wind nor storm,
Under the Bodhi Tree transformed.

The Evil Dybbuk

The dislocated
spirit of him crept inside
my body
by grabbing hold
a thin nostril hairline
fissure memory of grief.

A two cycle shift
Had long suffered
his oblong mouth.

I felt him there,
With his cowboy urban glare,
A hungry bellied ghost
easing into that
molded winter place for resting.

A yellow bag draped near
A silver dollar coin
To pass the void
With subtle expression.

My hair tangle clean
Over the porcelain tub
Into the water stream

releasing the black tar enigma
Where the grape bush tinged constructive terms
Through black diamond mud.

Loose leaf Egyptian lotus painted purple streaks
in the fine gold trimmed teacup.
It cracked as it fell,
From hyper tone
The ramen noodled strands
Dangled over the attempts to strangle out the
evil dybbuk
Draped lightweight about my neck.
Like a royal tunic.
But me thinks he's free now.
Or at least his stomach full.

This Time

My olfactory caught the
best of me
a scent of covid today,
in a glob of Al-coal-holic palmistry,
My black shoes,
Sees tar and feathered stars,
A fine fissure
    crack,
take one drag in
of the holy amber grain landscape.

It burnt my nose to a crisp,
Like the first tease of meth,
powder white pony
thunder gallops in
headquarters of lady liberty dimebag
pinch the nose off you know,
Jesse James style,
it gets you at the thumb,
Numb nomadic haze.
Drain down your
throat up chuck comet
Green scratch pad fade.

Spite that rolled up dollar dallup

a silver wonton badged medallion
o' daisy, right between the acne blister face,
like you do when Ol' St Nick's
Red pants pulled up past his waist,
Dont nobody find it weird
 they tell us to sit upright
on his strange old dirtball lap,
and whisper what toys he brings
for being good,
black boot Betty Boop,
like Nicholas sees us
in our birthday tie dyed suits
no pip it aint that slit up your dress
confess which mattel plastic get up
you want blessed.

Im tired Mammy,
Your hanker-chief
headdress stolen
like a brave old man
whose horses sold at trading post for land
at summertime,
filled up to the brim with wheat field cotton corn
cob
cotton candy
carnivale raped red
wizard fumes
this gay ol' time is making me
confused. Clockwerk orange brown

tower, over them til mad hits,
I just want the twinkle tree maggots,
To leave me bee,
But the Angelican in me
Wont let me sin real nice
He knocked three times on the pipe
And Grand,
Mama got ran over
by the sandman,
Ive grown a fan
Of Arabian baseball fertility rituals.
Knock it off and look normal
Outta the park this time.

From Poor Cotton Stitch

When it was evening,
Summer sun grew later
Larger near the
orange-pink horizon
of a kindled phase
As a tattered dress
With frayed strings
from poor cotton stitch
clung to the tired ankles
Of an expectant mother
Her eighth time around.

The whispers of the townspeople
Wondering where she gets her gumption
Wondering where she gets her stubborn
Enough to evoke the higher realms
of Angelic regimes to fight
those plucking strings
vibrate against the owlish
     cause within the night.

Hanging another dingy white,
eggshell of a baby cloth,
On the wire to dry,
Her biggest toe is sloshed with,

Suds of soap,
From the wooden basin,
After the cardinal lacks,
Enough vigorous strength,
To land upright.

It had been the fall,
From an elevated height,
A baptism from mire and dirt
That helped the goads along.
The plough of Nandi
Encircled the grains
For cakes and for yet sold

Sadness only envelopes
the objectification of time,
the sticks of butter,
the loaves of bread,
And the noontime whistles
That suggest the explosive
Blackness draws nearer to us
And each and every ear,
As we wait upon that old oak log
Far too quickly.

The Noisy Miner Bird's Song

The rooks in my
kingdom sing from the
darkest indigo past
a balm to ailing bones these starlings
almond bloomed branch perch
kiss Aurora's window
swelling over sun kindled cast
scaling power
strength, light. Gems upon
my balance weigh me down
a sapphire haze
definition rises as the dawning
Sun calls out to dusted walls
inside this fortress.
named
from my yellow, jaded
waxing moonlit path.

Near the Swan Marsh Lands I Call My Native Home

My palette is of the water's edge of China's
Sorrow,
The coolness of the keeps of Loch Lomond,
Pebbles near the pavement of the Seine,
A stone near the cliffs of Iona shore at dawn.

My hands hold the leaf branched veins of
Ghana,
The blue light lotus of the river Nile long,
My feet dance the pads of English pastures,
My hair blows with breeze to Ethiopian winded
song.
My eyes, almond round beneath the crescent
moon of Arabia.

My lips, the fertile soil red of Vietnam.
My strength from the mighty Blackfoot
Cherokee warriors of my name,
I rest my head near the muddy streams of the
Missouri River, near the swan marsh lands I call
my Native home.

The Gate Called Beauty

"I come to the garden alone
While the dew is still on the roses
And the voice I hear falling on my ear"

"Shitfire! Terri Lynn, get your n*gger kid off my
fence!"
We was just two little kids,
Playing out in our own back yard,
When that old neighbor lady's nose
Pushed her dirt screen out
To yell that name out loud at us
From her kitchen sink winda'

Old lady Keener had already
Told my Momma to move
Our swing set away from her gaze
She didn't wanna have to see
Two little black kids
Playin' from her yard

My brother's skin
Darker than mine
Held the heat of summer
Cut off denim shorts
Stark contrast white

cotton fibers danglin' down
Against his seven-year-old
eager black thighs

He had been chasin' after
A blue butterfly
The eastern blue tailed kind,
And I had been listening to the radio
Dancin' in my patent leather shoes
Beneath the tallest Persian Walnut tree
You could see for miles

It was Eden to us
Before the serpent filled us up
With wisdom from a paper cup
Made us eat that damn poison
That coal dung tar
Shoved down our throats
Making us think we needed a white Savior
His dripping blood
To cover our cursed skin
We had been prayed over
By Masonic men
Who thought just maybe
heaven might hold
A place for two colored kin.

But what about the Arabic
Tongues of our father's men?

Spread from Ethiopia to Ghana?
Would they just be considered unread djinn,
Field hands that had studied science
From Mali to Timbuktu
I was still learning to tie my shoes
Before I knew,
Thousands of years before the institutionalized
Whoredom said we were not beautiful.
That we needed to be covered
By slivers of ribah
Left wanting in the balance.

I stand at the gate
Called Beauty
Will ya'll let me in?
Will you take the blood sweat threads from these
hands?
Will you let me weave it on in?
The Kente cloth is much tighter now than it felt
back then,
Am I too light to carry the pained weight
Of a little girl with African curls
Straightened bone thin?

Momma, what did that lady call us?
Momma, what was that word?

Day of the Stranger

It is the day of the stranger.
Dark as the night that embraced us.
Neat as the whiskey we both took.
Poured into slim, tall glasses
Fogged by the chill of a winters age.
Poured out with a hint of French Masson.
A brandy grape that clouts my throat with bitter
sweetness.
A cigarette filled room as I awake.
I read the Psalms at his dying feet,
I hear the beating of his heart
In the refuge of my childrens' laughter.
A torquoise memory,
A feather weighs down my hand,
An urban cowboy paints near heaven's gates,
An action figure on my shelf.
Chiseled humans on vellum canvas,
He takes a seat at my table.
A chair, I left for him.

Lapis Lazuli

She wore his peace
Upon her eyes,
Gentle strokes
As dark as night
When the quiet descended upon
her shoulders
Like a shimmering, woven shawl.

When the waves of sorrow,
enveloped her with
strong arm drunkenness and
time shrouded memories
swelled pregnant beyond the chill
Of an Autumn grave filled fog.

She kept silence at her hip,
Like a ready-loaded holster,
Heavy coals left where diamonds
Once had softly laid
Now reaped from foreign hands
That gave stars away on loan.

She stole pieces of her own,
When the days grew long
When strength crept away into black holes

That wormed away
Weaving in and out of her memory.

Her gentle quiet turned to wandering
Screams of helpless fright
When the child she had wanted
Lost the beat of its drum
And left her peace swimming
In a shallow haze.

Near Withered Cheek

Have you kissed towards the mirrored
reflection of your smile near
withered cheek?

Have the salt wounds of bitterness healed
of the hatred in your father's streets?
Did the wild cry of violence cease to pierce
the silent night?

Or has the fallen man descent of Africa
cause you too much heighted fright?
Did you ever sit to hear Mother Moses'
ancestral story beats?
Did you hear her legend stories of heartache
and wash her tired feet?

Are the streets of your Third District cleared
pristine as time before?
Are the Boulevards yet kept from relinquished
littered floors?
Have you offered hands to the youth
who pursue uncharted paths?

Have you rested or just
kept quiet and mindfully

just sat?
Have you as of late
swung upon the swings
of youth at Loose Park?

Have you heard the songs
of Jazz play near
18th & Vine at dark?
I'd suggest you continue to thrive
among the best of Kansas City's art.

Continue to paint words of justice
do not forget
where you had start.
Bring the tired, bring the hurt,
together as time passed,
Have them bleed out with
their pen in hand,
their sorrow on streets
without gun in tow,
Do not forget to see a movie,
Take yourself out to a good old-fashioned show.

On days when you are saddened,
And on days when it is hard,
Remember the sun still shines
on you and that I brought this greeting card.

Between Parallel Spaces

My life's design,
Rippled between parallel spaces,
Black fades to grey,
My fingers entwine,
Combed within the stranded lines,
Of my now paling hair.

The baptismal waters wrenched
between my tired phalanx bones.
Bent over,
I douse my head
in the wells of Zamzam.

I stand East of the Ka'aba,
Beside Aisha,
Higher than the Ummayid could loft,
For the raven's nest has fallen upon the floors of
discontent.

My view is upon that Mountain,
That one that lifts Judas
from the red budded tree,
Pilgrim's Progress shoved
a laurel wreath around my neck,
The noose supplanted.

The salt has spilled,
As the milk evaporates from my opened meat
filled mouth,
I am struck by the vertical reality that
reverberates,
From the bitterness of the
stolen melanization from our cells.

The very reversing of our chromosomes,
We are not defined,
By the confinement,
Of their hatred for our Spirit:

We must,
We must,
We must,
Let them breathe,
Through Us.

Melting Chocolate: A Haibun

I believe it was 1987.
I was five years old.
The rain that night was beating down in
drenches, pouring down fiercely outside.
I saw the pouring through the kitchen window of
our door, beyond the white, curtains parted.

We lived near the train tracks and so the sound
of a train always calls out to me in the timbre of
a man's voice; because that night was distinct.
That night she sat us down, Adam on one side of
her, me on the other.

Slowly, she reckoned the truth of it all to us.
That he was not our father.
That we were black children.
Different than all the other children we lived
amongst.
That what we had known was not entirely true,
had been foraged out of some sense of
protection.

Protection from what?

As perfection of a justified tongue was beaten
into us from the start,
I'd realize later that it wasn't beaten into us, this
proper tongue.
That our tongue, our native rite, was beaten out
of us.
For whose protection,
I still don't know.

Melting chocolate;
Deep, even tones of a man,
Belton, Missouri.

Lufthansa

The smell of rose water,
Dissolves into the back of my nose,
Fragrant petals,
Fallen from a ground shift subsidence.

A ticking time clock,
Shift shaped into freedom,
A forced chitchat splatter,
The strengthened biceps,
Of a man torn from his cradle,
Offer me comfort.
If not even rest.

As bombs of misfortune,
Drape like a canopy over our heads,
The women veiled in a midnight fortress,
Paled soft shadows enhance the dread,
From an arsenal savior of capitalist martyrdom.

A worn fabric of crimson and blue toes,
Uncovered to frost bitten madness,
The liberty bell cracked from a sunken night,
In a Tehrani bed.

Nobody fawns for second best,

It is time to clean the vomit,
From the Cheshire's vest,
Wave the flagship,
In left keeled detour,
The squirrels offer no meat,
'Cept bubonic plague.

True Alchemy

A defiantly deviated cat,
The sinister of my heart's chambers
are not quite the same
breathing pattern of a man's.

Kali stands upon Shiva,
With his bloody severed head within her hands,
We only deflect our realities.
And I must say something about mirrors:
Stay away from them.
Doesn't yours have an opaque blackness behind
it?

The mad Arab runs within my veins,
Maybe that's the difference of being clever
between you and I.
I've been quantified as such.
Once you are able to let a lady go first, you'll
achieve the world.

But I'm not quantified a lady,
For I am rather vulgar.
All is fair in being human.
And I am an ambassador of diplomacy.

The programmed tapes run amok
when they choose to sniff the air.
Like even now,
I smell coconuts,
Me thinks she's mad;
Oh, she's definitely mad,
Cuckoo for cocoa nuts.
Chocolatey goodness.

Which reminds me of Gilda Radner,
Or maybe her dead husband.
And yes, I know I was being punny;
Which Latin abuses the difference:
P is Latin while F is, well...
P is soft in music.
And I forget that I am quite loud,
I think Manson might have been misunderstood.
For he must have played with mirrors,
I've swam the waters of reflecting light,
I'd caution them as well.

For I've stood at such an abyss,
They exist, but the reality of such fairy tail is
quite a Grimm's opus.
That's why you should caution playing near and
dear to mirrors.

My brother died of liver cancer,
Never was a drinker,

Those unfortunate genes,
Threaded knots of dreaded curses.

True Alchemy requires a water bath basin,
It is the outside that begs our distractions,
I have awakened the Mummy.

Madness makes a voyeur display of us all.
Dissipated boredom,
I enjoy a nice insanity once in awhile.

The English tongue is a whore.
Pure exploited craftiness,
The various mother languages
are flipped off in the effort to communicate.

This sovereign harlot likes
to get her way while playing the coy nun,
She's stolen all the dingle berries
from every ass crack
in the time space continuum
while sparing time for midday tea.

Black Faced Doll

Black faced doll
chubby porcelain cheeked
cloth antique white sleeved
sad idle on a shelf
dusty attic cleaned
painted chestnut eyes
catch winter madness scenes
golden bonnet girl
ten countess fertile fiend
tossed to and fro by no man
estate established by such dreams.

Head First

I had woke to fear in my throat.
Clinging to a Bible,
Whose pages, white with envy,
Soothed like a baleful lullaby.
I blinked back darkness,
Clawing against darklit halls,
Mirrors that gave back
Generous glances of felo de ce..
Hangings like a bell tolled
    pendulum fancy plagued my
brain's excursion to an altered space,
Caught up between there and along
the slithering pass near Liffey River,
On the ides of March.
The night wrenched of sleep
As I begged questions of why
From my father, the end of an era.
I stepped largely near the cliffs of insanity, then
dove in,
Head first.

Coggleshall Farm

They begged masks of us
To sally protection
Pageantry for the masses
Doctoral aggression
The seeping of swan moss
sands, tiny crystal ball lands
Loosed bands carry
enveloped existence
postage stamp cadusa mistress
Unseen by the naked eye
Fishing with synch
Line and hooks
Worm hole illusions
Intrusions upon bile
ducts metallic
lined water
Ways, Piped nightmares
plastic placated wares
Spigots for the hungry ghosts
The stench of ascension
Dried tongues
Bitter budded boards
Leather grime
To scrape the mucous edge off
They begged fear of us

A coagulating curse
Shut up in tiny houses
Here comes your hearse
Quantum currencies
Line the halls of a Coggelshall Farm
The white flag has flown it's
Tattered cords
In the place of the one
That shrouds the aborted
Babies' umbilicals
 With it's red,
Then white,
Now Boo!
Betsy Ross
Eat your heart out
Yale and Harvard too
They teach us these colors
A thimble full of blood
I know what's in
The midwife's late night
TV dinner.
No need for a second layer
Masquerade ball already,
A lady in waiting
Wasted, hiding
our bloated apple dumplin'
Faces.
It puts the mask on
Or it gets

The non binary
Hose.

On Night Time Terror

I think she floated above you
before the anxiety attack
with claws of a bird
draping raven hair that was
too long for even her.

She, with alabaster skin
let the hair drape over
your frame as you slept,
watching you like
an owlet screeching cherub,
before distorting your peaceful slumber
into a frequency that is only
disclosed between 3am and 5.

The the basal body temperature
fevers awaken you into a cold, death stare.
During this time, the conjuring
isn't of your will, but her own.

She creeps between the
silent floorboards passed the august moons
of the witching hours.
We don't get to conjure her,
she is our ancestors' nightmare,

drudging the silver chains
of our abandoned freedom
until we wake from our void
into our colorful inheritance.

She doesn't hold our future,
only the ability
to harden hearts.
Time isn't her engagement.
I've stared into
those abysmal ferrofluids,
Pharoah fluids of my fathers lineage.

Ramses the 3rd
and what I know flows out
into the sarcophagus and its
splintered wooden vats
I still know we can scream no
against the bitter angst that throbs
against the membranes of our hearts.

When we awaken to
the golden sphere that
can dispell the echo of calamity
it is then we know not her name, but our own.

A Persian King's Way

He asked her to tea,
Of a parched tongue she lept
Into the hollow,
Her eyes full of wonder,
Her mind spinning as she crept.

The burden of ignorance
Slung at her arm
Like a green colored knapsack.

The walls of his chambers
Lacked the naked scent of peace.
Where brilliant colors blurred the
Ambrosia rug filled scene.

The depths of Stephen's rose
In height of full bloom sight
When wavering in focus
Took a path long laid in spite.

Through wooded forest and
Through leveled moss filled roads
The grape vine of an Eastern King arose.

It grew along a meadow

Near fields of yellowed grass
Near country folk who carried on
As if they killed a fatted calf.

When awakened upon the sunlight as the moon
Took time to hide
The world lost a precious amount and
relinguished
Its stolen pride.

Now as the children play
On a winter wonder land
The tunnels of his castle keep
Turned up exposed of blown away dune sands.

As time will tell the story of the King and his
Fleur de lis, he leads her on a journey built
upon a sonnet spring.

www.ingramcontent.com/pod-product-compliance
Lightning Source LLC
Chambersburg PA
CBHW070611160726

48003CB00005B/2216